D1742800

H£3 30
9C

Holmes McDougall: History 11-13

Studies in Evidence 2

The Battle of Hastings

Terry Lewis

**General Editor:
Ian Dawson**

Contents

Design by Pat Macdonald

Artwork by Harry Trowell, David Wilson and Denby Designs

ISBN 0 7157 2138-0

© Terry Lewis 1987. Printed and published by Holmes McDougall Ltd., Allander House, 137-141 Leith Walk, Edinburgh EH6 8NS.

Front cover: *Part of the Bayeux Tapestry, by courtesy of the town of Bayeux.*

1: Introduction

The most famous battle in English history

All schoolchildren have probably heard of the Battle of Hastings. Many know quite a lot about the battle. Can you answer these five questions?

When was the battle fought?
Where was the battle fought?
Who fought the battle?
Who won the battle?
What happened to the loser?

If you are not sure of the answers you will find help from the source on this page. This is the first page of a history book used over 100 years ago. Children had to learn all the facts about English history — including the Battle of Hastings — by heart.

ENGLISH HISTORY.

WILLIAM THE CONQUEROR

Ascended the throne in 1066, died in 1087, after a reign of 21 years.

1. *Who was William the Conqueror?*
William the Conqueror was Duke of Normandy. He invaded England in the year 1066, fought a memorable battle near Hastings in Sussex, where King Harold was killed, and William succeeded to his throne.

2. *Did William enjoy a peaceable Reign?*
No: William was almost constantly engaged in war with the neighbouring nations, and even his own children conspired against him.

This book is going to help you find out more about the Battle of Hastings but you probably won't have to learn it by heart. You have already answered five questions about the battle. What other questions do you want to ask about 'the most famous battle in English history'?

Your questions are probably quite like the questions below. If you can find the answers to these questions you will know a lot more about the Battle of Hastings. You will understand why the battle was fought and how William defeated Harold and conquered England.

1　How did the Norman and Saxon armies prepare for the battle?
2　How did the battle start?
3　What methods of fighting were used?
4　How did King Harold die?
5　Why did the Normans win the battle?
6　Why did the Normans invade England?

Finding the answers won't always be easy. Everybody has heard of the Battle of Hastings but people have different ideas about it. Look at the pictures on these pages — what differences can you see in the pictures?

a: *The first known painting of the Battle of Hastings.*

b: *An illustration from Hollinshed's 'Chronicle', drawn in 1577.*

c: *A modern reconstruction of the battle.*

Now that you have looked closely at the pictures
— which of them gives you the best idea of what the battle was like?
— why do you think that one is more accurate than the others?

2 : Sources – Relics of the Battle

How do we know about the battle?

Did you decide that picture C gives the best idea of the battle? If you did, you were right! The artist who drew picture C was more accurate because he used his *sources* carefully. Historians (whether they are writers or artists) base their work on sources left from the past. They use these sources as evidence to answer their questions. Artist C used his sources as evidence of what happened at Hastings. What kinds of sources did he use?

You may already have learned about sources called 'relics' — the things left from the past by accident, such as tools, weapons and even housing. These relics are made of stone, metal, bone or wood, which are all materials that last through the centuries.

Opposite: *Two views over the battle site. The top one shows Battle Abbey, which was built by William to commemorate the victory and marks the site of Harold's command post.*

The battlefield

What kinds of relics will help us to find out about the Battle of Hastings? One student wrote, 'If we excavate the battlefield, we might find armour and weapons which were used in the battle and perhaps some other artefacts like coins and jewellery.' The student mentions several different kinds of relics, including the battlefield itself. Do we know where the battlefield is? Fortunately, William the Conqueror decided to give thanks to God for the victory and he ordered that an abbey be built on the site where Harold was killed. Nowadays it is possible to visit the battlefield and the town of Battle that has grown up near the abbey.

Look carefully at the pictures of the battlefield on this page. Do you think the battlefield gives us any information to answer our questions? Can you work out why it is difficult to use the battlefield, as it is today, to decide what happened over 900 years ago?

Weapons and armour

The battlefield does not help to answer our questions by itself. You could spend days walking around it but you would still need to look for information in other sources. If you remember, the student hoped to find other relics on the battlefield, but no relics — swords or helmets or axes — have ever been found on the battlefield. Why not? What happened to those valuable weapons that must have been on the battlefield?

Looking in other places

Although there are no relics from Hastings we can look elsewhere for them. Historians have found relics from that time in other places. On this page you can see some of these relics. Do they help to answer our questions?

Left top: *Sword, axe head and shield boss.* Left bottom: *Iron weapons.* Right: *Norman knights wearing chain mail, also shows helm and shields.*

These relics might be very useful. They could help to answer the questions about the methods of fighting. But how do we prove that these are the same kinds of weapons as were used at Hastings? To do this we need to look at another source — the Bayeux Tapestry.

The Bayeux Tapestry was made soon after the battle. It tells the story of the Norman conquest of England and tells us a lot about the battle. Does it help us to decide whether the relics shown on page 8 are the kinds of weapons used in the battle?

You can see these kinds of weapons very clearly in the tapestry. Using more than one source is very important. We cannot learn much from the battlefield alone or from the relics found in other places, but if we use them together with other sources we can learn a lot. If you look closely at the Bayeux Tapestry you should even be able to work out why there were no relics left on the battlefield.

Right: *Leofwine and Gyrth, Harold's brothers, fought on foot.*

Below: *King Harold is killed.*

9

Records — a new kind of source

The swords and helmets that have survived from the past are called relics. They are accidental remains — nobody expected them to survive. The Bayeux Tapestry is a different kind of source. It was made deliberately to tell the story of the Norman Conquest — to *record* what happened. We call sources that were written or drawn by people who wanted to collect information *records*. Historians use the information in records as evidence to answer their questions.

Two kinds of sources

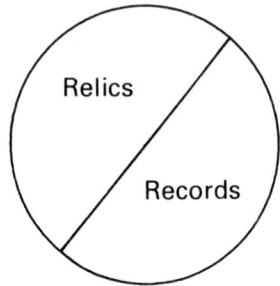

Information and evidence

Sources contain information, e.g. people stole armour and weapons from the dead after the Battle of Hastings.

   Historians use this information as evidence to answer their questions, e.g. Why aren't there any relics at Hastings?

   Answer:

   'There aren't any relics because the weapons were stolen.'

   The Bayeux Tapestry shows pictures of this happening — evidence.

Early records in England

People have been making records since man first learned to write. In England, long before the Battle of Hastings, records were being written and drawn. Many of these records have been lost or destroyed over the centuries but some have survived. They tell us a lot about the sorts of people who wrote them and the way that records were written.

A section of Bede's 'History of the English Church and People'.

10

The Lindisfarne Gospel.

Most of the early records were written by monks and churchmen. For example, we have the beautiful Lindisfarne Gospels, probably written about AD 700 by the monk Eadfrith. Many of these records were written in Latin, which was the language of the church for hundreds of years. They were often beautifully and colourfully decorated, or illuminated, with designs in the letters at the starts of the chapters.

Kings quickly realised that written records were useful. They began libraries at monasteries. Soon they employed monks as clerks to write down all sorts of information about their laws and their activities. The monks also wrote 'histories', which recorded events in the order in which they happened. The most famous of these monastic writers was Bede (AD 673–735) who wrote a *History of the English Church and People.*

When Alfred became king in 871 he soon saw the problems of having all the records written in Latin. This was a language that few of his subjects understood. So during his reign Alfred had churchmen translate many records into Anglo-Saxon, the language of the ordinary people at that time.

The *Anglo-Saxon Chronicle* — one of the most important records in all of English history — was started during Alfred's reign. It is possible that Alfred himself may have ordered the monks to begin writing it. The *Anglo-Saxon Chronicle* continued long after Alfred's death. It gives us a record of Anglo-Saxon times for over 250 years, until 1154, when it was ended. The *Anglo-Saxon Chronicle* was copied many times. Some of the copies give different accounts of what happened. In the *Anglo-Saxon Chronicle* is a record of the Norman Conquest and the Battle of Hastings.

Translation of Anglo-Saxon Chronicle

And King Harold his brother assembled a naval force and a land force larger than any king had assembled before in this country, because he had been told that William the Bastard meant to come here and conquer this country. This was exactly what happened afterwards. Meanwhile Earl Tosti came into the Humber with 60 ships and Earl Edwin came with a land force and drove him out, and the sailors deserted him. And he went to Scotland with twelve small vessels, and there Harald, King of Norway, met him with three hundred ships, and Tosti submitted to him and became his vassal; and they both went up the Humber until they reached York.

From the Anglo-Saxon Chronicle. The marked text is translated above.

3: Sources – Records of the Battle

Not many people wrote about the Battle of Hastings. Only seven accounts were produced within 50 years of the battle. If this battle was so important, why do you think there are so few records of it?

Records produced soon after the Battle of Hastings

Record	Author/Chronicle	Date
The Bayeux Tapestry	We do not know who embroidered the tapestry but it was probably made for William's half-brother, Bishop Odo of Bayeux, who was present at the battle.	1067–1082
The Acts of the Norman Dukes	William of Jumieges, a Norman monk.	1070 or 1071
The Acts of William Duke of the Normans and King of the English	William of Poitiers, who was not present at the battle, but who was first a knight in the service of Duke William and then became his chaplain.	1071–1076
A poem to Adela, the Conqueror's daughter. The poem was largely based on Poitiers' work.	Baudri, Abbot of Bourguil	1099–1102
The Chronicle of Battle Abbey	Anonymous	First part before 1107
The Chronicle of Chronicles	Florence of Worcester, an English monk	Before 1118
The Anglo-Saxon Chronicle	Anonymous. The Chronicle was first begun in King Alfred's reign. There were several versions of the Chronicle. The one that gives details of Hastings is known as the D version.	The D version possibly not written until the 12th century

This table gives you the names of the most important records, some information about the writers and the dates when the records were produced.

Above: *Detail from the tapestry. If you look closely you can see that it is in fact an embroidery.*

Below left: *The Cathedral at Bayeux.*
Below right: *The tapestry as it is displayed in Bayeux today.*

Why do historians need to know
— who produced the source?
— how the writer got his information?
— when the source was produced?

Historians do not use just one source to answer a question. They need to use several sources together before they can find the answers. We are going to use these records to investigate the battle. We have already met one of them, the Bayeux Tapestry, which is one of the most famous records in English history.

The Bayeux Tapestry

No-one knows exactly when the Tapestry was made but it was produced within twenty years of the battle. For centuries it lay almost unknown in Bayeux Cathedral until historians discovered it in the early eighteenth century. From then on it gradually became more and more famous.

In 1803 Napoleon had the Tapestry taken to Paris. He was planning his own invasion of England, which, as we know, was not successful, and the Tapestry was returned to Bayeux Cathedral.

Bishop Odo of Bayeux, William's half-brother, probably ordered that the Tapestry should be made. The 'tapestry' is in fact an embroidery. It is a series of 79 linen panels joined together to tell of William's reasons for invasion, the invasion preparations, and the battle. The Bayeux Tapestry is a very special record of the Battle of Hastings because it contains both writing and illustration. A picture-story of the battle was made and Latin captions explain the pictures. Many people could not read in the eleventh century and so the picture-story was very important.

Now we know what sources we have for the battle. We have relics *and* records. The next four pages will help you to understand why records are so useful — and why you must use them with care.

Why are records so useful?

We have already used a record — the Bayeux Tapestry — to provide information about the battle. We used this information as evidence about the types of weapons used in the battle. However records have other uses. First, they can provide a lot more information than relics. Second, they can provide a different kind of information. Records tell us things that relics cannot.

On these pages are some extracts from records. What do they tell you that you could not learn from relics?

What did people wear?

a: *Count Guy took Harold to William.*

b: *Duke William with Harold.*

How did people behave?

c   'When he became King, Harold abolished bad laws and made good laws. He gave help to churches and monasteries and was religious and friendly to everyone. But he treated criminals with great severity and gave orders for all thieves and robbers to be imprisoned.'

(adapted from Florence of Worcester)

d   'From the third hour of the day until dusk, Harold bravely withstood the enemy, and fought so courageously and stubbornly that the enemy could make hardly any impression.

(adapted from Florence of Worcester)

e   'Seeing his own troops running away, William stood in front of them, shouting at them and threatening them with his spear. He took off his helmet and shouted "Look at me! I am alive and by the Grace of God I shall win the battle. You are throwing away victory. If you run away you will all be killed." '

(adapted from William of Poitiers)

Why did people do things?

f   'The English saw that they could not hold out much longer. They had lost most of their army. The King with his two brothers and many lords were dead. Those who were still alive were exhausted. They could get no more help so they began to escape as fast as they could.'

(adapted from William of Poitiers)

g   'After the battle William was met by the Archbishop and Prince Edgar, Earl Edwin and Earl Morcar and all the chief men from London. They submitted to William because they had no other choice.'

(adapted from the *Anglo-Saxon Chronicle*)

Relics could not answer these questions about people at the time of the battle. Records give us some answers, but we must be careful. Do we always believe what records tell us?

Do we believe records?

'Historians have an easy job. They just find the records and copy out what they say.' Do you agree with that? To see if historians have an easy job we will try to find out how many men were in the English army at Hastings. What does the Bayeux Tapestry tell us?

According to the Bayeux Tapestry, how many men were in the English army? Do you think this is correct?

Norman cavalry charge the Saxon wall of shields.

a 'King Harold assembled a large army and there were heavy casualties on both sides.' (adapted from the *Anglo-Saxon Chronicle*)

b 'The king at once marched with his army. He knew that some of the bravest Englishmen had already been killed in the battles against the Norwegians and that half his army had not yet arrived. However he did not hesitate to advance.'
(adapted from Florence of Worcester)

c 'William advanced bravely against the terrible army.'
(adapted from William of Jumieges)

d 'A noble lady sent a messenger to William saying "King Harold is hurrying towards you at the head of an innumerable army."'
(adapted from William of Poitiers)

e 'From all parts of England a vast army had gathered together.'
(adapted from William of Poitiers)

It is not easy to work out the size of the English army. Sometimes the records are vague, sometimes they exaggerate, sometimes — like the Bayeux Tapestry — they cannot tell the truth. So historians have to be careful. They do not just accept what the records tell them. This is why it is important to check sources against each other.

The rest of the book will help you to answer the six questions about the battle. This is your chance to use the sources as evidence.

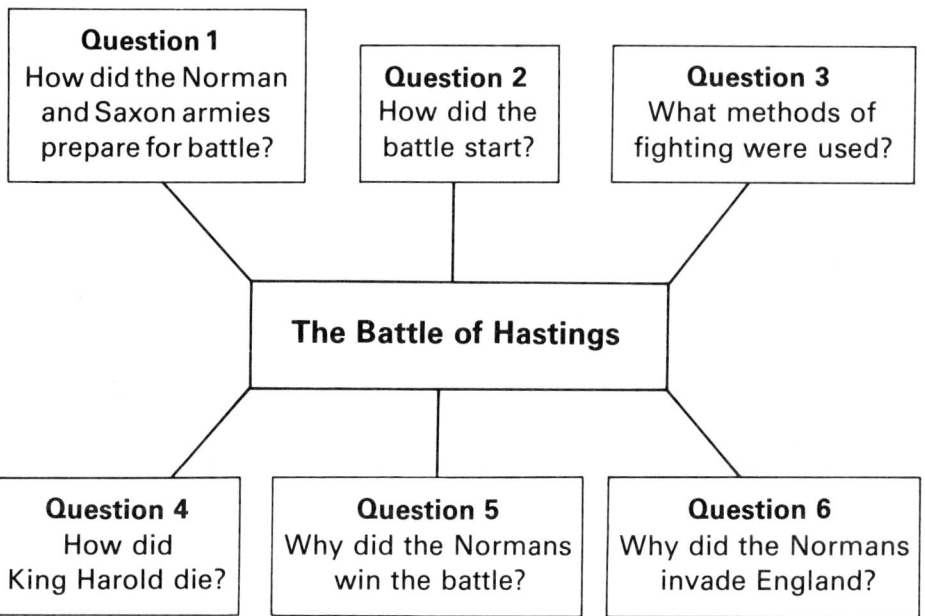

Question 1
How did the Norman and Saxon armies prepare for battle?

Question 2
How did the battle start?

Question 3
What methods of fighting were used?

The Battle of Hastings

Question 4
How did King Harold die?

Question 5
Why did the Normans win the battle?

Question 6
Why did the Normans invade England?

4 : Using the Sources as Evidence

How did the Norman and Anglo-Saxon armies prepare for the battle?

Using sources to support each other
To answer this question we can use the records together. Usually the records will support each other but sometimes a record will tell us something that none of the others mention. Then we have to decide whether or not to believe this new piece of information.

William's preparations
After William decided to invade England he collected his army. He promised that he would give English land to the knights in his army. This persuaded many soldiers to make the dangerous journey. William also won the support of the Pope by promising to improve the English church. This helped to persuade some Norman barons that the invasion was just and right.

William had many other things to do. These scenes from the Bayeux Tapestry show you his preparations.

A: *Flat-bottomed boats were built.*

If you are going to get a good answer to our question you must use the sources together. This grid will help you to find and check the information.

	Bayeux Tapestry	Support from other sources	New information not in Bayeux Tapestry
A	Flat-bottomed boats were built.	'The duke had ships built' (William of Poitiers)	'a fleet of 3000 ships' (William of Jumieges)
B	The boats were loaded with hauberks, swords, axes, spears, helmets, and barrels of supplies.		

In column 1 is a description of the scenes from the Tapestry. Column 2 has a quotation from another record that tells us the same thing. Column 3 contains other information that is in the written records but not in the Tapestry.

For Panel B, columns 2 and 3 have been left empty. Can you complete them, using the extracts below?

a 'William therefore hastily built a fleet of 3000 ships.'

(adapted from William of Jumieges)

b 'At\length he brought his fleet to anchor, where he filled it with mighty horses and most valiant men, with hauberks and helmets.'

(adapted from William of Jumieges)

B: *They carry weapons to the ships.*

On these pages are more extracts telling how the Normans prepared for the battle. Draw up a grid like the one on page 19 and decide for yourself what preparation the Normans made. This time you will have to work out for yourself what to put in column 1.

C: *To Pevensey.*

D: *They hurried to Hastings.*

E: *The Normans foraged for food.*

F: *The castle at Hastings.*

a 'The whole fleet waited for a long time for a south wind but was then blown by a west wind to the harbour of St. Valery. William, unshaken by the delay or the loss of ships or the desertion of some soldiers, prayed for the protection of heaven. At length the longed-for wind began to blow.'

(adapted from William of Poitiers)

b 'When a favourable wind began to blow William set sail and crossed the sea, landing at Pevensey.'

(adapted from William of Jumieges)

c 'Then Duke William came from Normandy to Pevensey on Michaelmas Eve (29th September).'

(adapted from *Anglo-Saxon Chronicle*)

d 'William left Pevensey in the charge of some troops and with others he hurried to Hastings.'

(adapted from William of Jumieges)

e 'the greater part of William's army had gone out foraging.'

(adapted from William of Poitiers)

f 'Harold was furious because he heard the Normans had ravaged the neighbourhood of their camp.'

(adapted from William of Poitiers)

g 'at Pevensey William immediately built a castle with a strong defence. He hurried to Hastings where he built another similar castle.'

(adapted from William of Jumieges)

By now you should know a lot about the Norman preparations. By using the records together you can learn more than you can from just one record. The Bayeux Tapestry gives us plenty of details, but we need to check it with the other sources and add new information.

Now, what about the Anglo-Saxons?

The English preparations

The Bayeux Tapestry tells us a lot about the Norman preparations because it tells the story of the Norman invasion. It does not show much of what was happening in England so it is better to start with an English source. To find out what was happening in England we can read the *Anglo-Saxon Chronicle*.

'King Edward died on 5th January and was buried in Westminster Abbey. And Earl Harold was crowned king and he met little quiet as long as he ruled the realm. Over all England a sign was seen in the shires such as had never been seen before. Some said it was the star 'comet' which some call the star with hair. It first appeared on 24 April and shone all the week.

King Harold gathered a naval force and a land force larger than had ever been assembled before in this country because he had been told as a fact that Duke William meant to come and conquer the country.

When his fleet was assembled he went to the Isle of Wight. He stayed there all that summer and a land force was kept everywhere along the sea, though in the end it was no use. By 8 September the food was gone and nobody could stay any longer. Then they were allowed to go home.

After this, Harald Hardrada, King of Norway, came by surprise with all his fleet up the Ouse towards York. There Earl Edwin and Earl Morcar fought against him but the Norwegians won. Then Harold came upon the Norwegians by surprise beyond York at Stamford Bridge. There was a very fierce fight and King Harald Hardrada of Norway was killed. The English were victorious.'

(adapted from *The Anglo-Saxon Chronicle*)

Left: *The burial of King Edward.*

Right: *These people wondered at the star.*

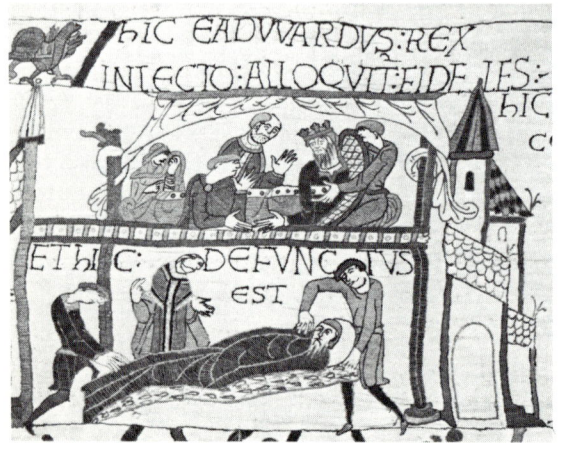

In this grid the main points in the *Anglo-Saxon Chronicle* are listed in the left-hand column. Do the records on page 22 and this page support the information in the *Anglo-Saxon Chronicle*? Do they provide any new information?

Anglo-Saxon Chronicle	Support from other records	New information
Harold crowned. 'Long-haired' star seen. King Harold assembled a large navy and army.		
Harald Hardrada, King of Norway, invaded Yorkshire.		
King Harold marched north and won a great victory at Stamford.		
News arrived of the Norman landing. The English marched south.		

The map on the inside front cover shows Harold's march to Yorkshire and back to Pevensey.

'On 5th January King Edward died and Harold was chosen king. On 24 April a comet was seen and it shone for seven days. As Duke William was preparing to invade England he waited all summer with his army and navy. But about 8 September food fell short so the forces returned home. After this Harald Hardrada arrived suddenly and sailed up the Ouse. Before King Harald's arrival the two brother-earls, Edwin and Morcar, fought a battle on 20th September with the Norwegians but after a long contest the English fled. Five days after this Harold king of the English killed King Harald of Norway and gained a complete victory. In the middle of this when the king might have thought all his enemies were beaten he was told that William had landed at Pevensey.'

(adapted from Florence of Worcester)

By now you have looked at how both armies prepared for battle. Which army was better prepared: the Normans, carefully organised by William, or the Anglo-Saxons, who had already won a great victory?

This chapter has helped you to use the records together. Often different records say the same things. Sometimes a piece of information can be found in only one record and then we must be especially careful in deciding whether or not to believe it.

How did the battle start?

Do sources always lead to the same conclusions?

In the last chapter you answered the question, 'How did the two armies prepare for the battle?' The records usually agreed with each other and this made it easier to answer the question. But what happens when sources are vague or even disagree with each other? This is the problem you will have when you try to answer the next question, 'How did the battle start?'

The battle took place on 14 October. By then the Normans had been in England for over two weeks and were well prepared. Harold and his army had won the Battle of Stamford Bridge on 25 September, when they had taken the Norwegians by surprise, and then they had to march south to Pevensey, where William had landed. The English army was not as strong as it had been because many men had been killed and many more were probably very tired after the long march south.

Historians have suggested that the battle may have started in three different ways:

1 Harold chose a narrow, hilltop position for strong defence and he forced the Normans to attack him.

2 William took Harold by surprise before the English were ready.

3 The battle started as soon as the two sides saw each other.

By looking at the sources on the next three pages you should be able to decide which of these answers you agree with.

Plan of the battlefield site.

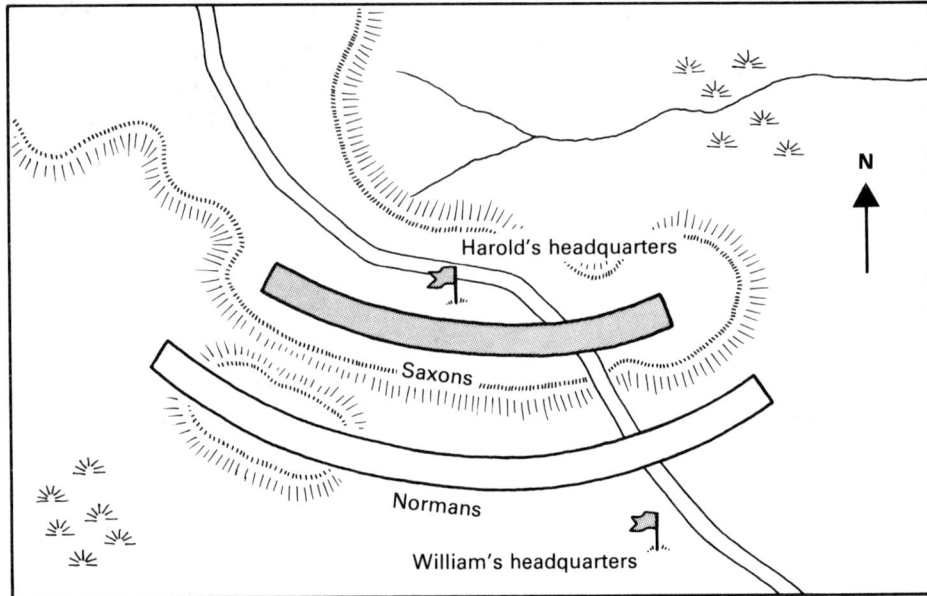

24

Some definite answers

Some of our sources seem very helpful. On this page you can see those that seem to point definitely to one answer. But they do not agree with each other!

'and William came against him by surprise before his army was drawn up in battle array.'

(Anglo-Saxon Chronicle)

Which source suggests that Harold was taken by surprise? Which show that the English position was very strong? The sources disagree. Perhaps we ought to look at some more?

On these pages are more sources that help to answer the question, 'How did the battle start?' Look at each one carefully. Does it support one of the three possible answers? Sometimes sources may not clearly support one answer but they may rule out another.

1   Harold chose a narrow, hilltop position for a strong defence and he forced the Normans to attack him.

2   William took Harold by surprise before the English were ready.

3   The battle started as soon as the two sides saw each other.

a   'Harold knew very well that some of the bravest men in all England had fallen in the two battles against the Norwegians and that half his army was not yet assembled. Yet he did not hesitate to meet his enemy as quickly as he could, and nine miles from Hastings he joined battle with them before a third of his army was in order. But because the English were drawn up in a narrow place, many retired from the ranks, and very few remained true to him.'

(adapted from Florence of Worcester)

b: *Duke William asks Vidal (his scout)
if he has seen Harold.*

c: *He tells Duke William that he has seen Harold.*

d 'Harold, rejecting caution, advanced and, after riding all the night, he appeared on the field of battle early in the morning. But the duke had taken precautions against night-attacks by the enemy, and as the darkness approached he told his men to stand by until dawn. At first light, having placed his troops in three lines of battle, William advanced fearlessly against the terrible enemy.'

(adapted from William of Jumieges)

e 'In the meantime trusty knights who had been sent out by the duke on patrol came back in haste to report the approach of the enemy. Harold was furious because he had heard that the Normans had laid waste the neighbourhood of their camp, and he planned to take them unawares by a surprise or night attack. . .

'William then advanced in good order. In the front he placed foot soldiers equipped with arrows and crossbows; in the second rank came the more heavily armed infantry clad in hauberks, and finally came the squadrons of knights in the midst of whom he rode himself. . .'

(adapted from William of Poitiers)

What is *your* answer to the question 'How did the battle start?' Which sources support your view?

What methods of fighting were used?

So far you have been learning how to use records — checking whether they agree with each other and deciding whether to use them when they are vague or they disagree. You have been helped by questions and grids. This chapter gives you just the records. You must work out for yourself the answer to the question, 'What methods of fighting were used?'

The Norman army

a   'In the front William placed foot soldiers with arrows and crossbows. In the second rank came the more heavily armed infantry clad in hauberks, and finally came the squadrons of knights, in the midst of whom he rode himself so that he could give his orders by hand or voice.'

(adapted from William of Poitiers)

b   'At first light, having placed his troops in three lines of battle William advanced fearlessly against the terrible enemy.'

(adapted from William of Jumieges)

c   'William arrived with a countless host of horsemen, slingers, archers and foot soldiers.'

(adapted from Florence of Worcester)

d: *William gives the order to go into battle.*

28

e: *The Normans go into battle.*

f: *The Norman cavalry charges.*

The English army

a 'Fearing Duke William and not daring to fight with him on equal terms the English took up their position on higher ground, on a hill next to the forest. Dismounting from their horses they lined themselves up on foot and in very close order.'

(adapted from William of Poitiers)

b 'The English resisted valiantly, each man according to his strength. They hurled back spears and javelins and weapons of all kinds, together with axes and stones tied to pieces of wood.'

(adapted from William of Poitiers)

c 'The English fought confidently with all their strength, attempting to stop the Normans getting within their lines, which were indeed so closely packed that even the dead didn't have space to fall.'

(adapted from William of Poitiers)

d: *Harold's brothers are killed fighting on foot.*

Now you should know what kinds of soldiers were in the two armies and what kinds of weapons they had. You may also have worked out what formations they fought in. Do you think one side was better equipped than the other or were they about equal?

How did King Harold die?

Sources can be difficult to interpret

The Battle of Hastings was long and hard. It seems to have lasted most of the day as the two armies were well matched. Both leaders were very brave but when Harold was killed the battle was decided. The death of Harold is one of the things that nearly everyone has heard of. Harold was killed by an arrow in the eye.

But is that really what happened? What do the records tell us?

a 'Harold himself fighting amidst the front rank of his army, fell covered with deadly wounds.'

(adapted from William of Jumieges)

b 'and there were heavy casualties on both sides. King Harold was killed and Earl Leofwine his brother, and Earl Gyrth his brother, and many good men.'

(adapted from *Anglo-Saxon Chronicle*)

c 'at last, after great slaughter on both sides, about twilight, the king, alas, fell.'

(adapted from Florence of Worcester)

d 'The two brothers of King Harold were found near him, and Harold himself, stripped of all badges of honour, could not be identified by his face, but only by certain marks on his body.'

(adapted from William of Poitiers)

None of these records says that Harold was shot in the eye. But does that mean that he was not?

Do these records
1. support the 'arrow in the eye' story?
2. prove the 'arrow in the eye' story is wrong?
3. suggest that Harold might have been shot in the eye?

King Harold is killed.

If we look at the Bayeux Tapestry we seem to have clear evidence.

In the middle of this scene are two soldiers being killed. One seems to have been hit by an arrow, perhaps in his eye. The other is being struck down by the sword of a mounted knight. Above this scene the caption says 'Here King Harold is killed'. Which figure is King Harold? Could *both* men be Harold — being shot first, then struck down with a sword?

How do *you* think King Harold was killed? Could the 'arrow in the eye' story be true? Whatever the answer is, we can be certain of one thing. Our records are not always as clear as we would like them to be.

Representation of Harold's death drawn in the 1950s.

Why did the Normans win the battle?

Historians can draw conclusions that are not exactly stated in the sources. Harold's death finally decided the battle. But even before this, it seems that the Normans were winning. Harold was standing in the middle of his army. To kill him the Normans must have overcome many English soldiers.

Yet Harold's death is only part of the answer to the question, 'Why did the Normans win the battle?' To complete the answer we must see what happened during the battle. We know it was a long battle.

a   'The English were drawn up in a narrow place, many returned from the ranks and very few remained true to him. Nevertheless from the third hour until dusk Harold bravely withstood the enemy, and fought so valiantly and stubbornly in his own defence that the enemy's force could make hardly any impression.'

(adapted from Florence of Worcester)

b   'At first light Duke William advanced fearlessly against the terrible enemy. The battle began at the third hour of the day and continued with much bloodshed until nightfall.'

(adapted from William of Jumièges)

During such a long battle the two leaders had the chance to prove that they were good generals. Did the Normans win because William was a better general than Harold? This chapter gives you the chance to find out. The records won't tell you the answer directly. You will have to work it out from what happened.

Was William a better general than Harold?

Events	Harold	Source	William	Source
Before the battle	Harold won a great victory over the Norwegians by surprising their army.	Anglo-Saxon Chronicle	William collected and prepared a strong army and navy.	Bayeux Tapestry

Events	Harold	Source	William	Source
	He marched his army south at great speed to meet the Normans.	Florence of Worcester William of Jumieges	He kept them together despite a long delay.	William of Poitiers
	He took up a good defensive position on a hill.	Bayeux Tapestry William of Poitiers	The Normans landed safely and built a castle for defence.	William of Jumieges
The start of the battle	The battle began before Harold's army was at full strength.	Florence of Worcester	William and his army carefully arranged when the battle began.	William of Poitiers William of Jumieges
The first Norman attack				
The Norman retreat				
William's speech/actions				
English pursuers killed				
Mock flight by Normans				
Final attack on the English				

At the top of the grid are some of the events that happened before the battle. Do they suggest that Harold and/or William were good generals? During the battle there were six incidents for you to look at. If you fill in your conclusions on a grid like this it will help you to decide whether William was a better general than Harold.

The Normans attack — and retreat

Events	Harold	Source	William	Source
The first Norman attack				
The Norman retreat				

'William and his men, not at all dismayed by the difficulty of the ground, came slowly up the hill, and the terrible sound of trumpets on both sides signalled the beginning of the battle. The bravery of the Normans gave them the first advantage. The Norman footsoldiers rushed forward, wounding and killing the English with their weapons. The English fought back bravely, hurled back spears and javelins and dealt savage blows with their axes. Then the knights rode forward, eager to use their swords. The shouts of the two armies could hardly be heard for the clang of the weapons and the groans of the dying. For a long time the battle raged fiercely. The English had the advantage of the high ground. They bravely withstood the Normans, whether they were attacked at close quarters or shot at from a distance. Then the Norman footsoldiers, terrified by the violence of the battle, turned and ran and so did the knights from Brittany. The whole of the Duke's army was in danger of retreat.'

(adapted from William of Poitiers)

Saxon foot soldiers and Norman cavalry men fell together.

The tide turns

Events	Harold	Source	William	Source
William's speech/actions				
English pursuers killed				

'The Normans believed that the duke had been killed. Their flight was nothing to be ashamed of, they thought they had lost their leader.

'Seeing a large part of the enemy chasing his own troops, William thrust himself in front of his retreating troops, blocking those who were running away, shouting at them and threatening them with his spear. He took off his helmet and shouted "Look at me! I am still alive. With God's help I shall win! What madness makes you run away? If you run you will certainly be killed. You are throwing away victory and glory that will last for ever." With these words he restored their courage. Thundering forward with his sword he slaughtered the enemy. The Normans returned to the battle, surrounded the thousands who had chased them and rapidly cut them down so there wasn't a single survivor.'

(adapted from William of Poitiers)

Here is Duke William.

The Norman victory

Events	Harold	Source	William	Source
Mock flight by Normans				
Final attack on the English				

'Heartened by their success the Normans attacked the enemy with great violence but the English army seemed as big as ever. The English fought bravely with all their strength. The Normans realised that they would never overcome the enemy without great losses. Therefore they turned away, pretending to run away. They remembered that only a short time before their retreat had turned into a success. The barbarians thought they were winning and shouted with triumph, hurling insults at our men. As before several thousands of the English rushed forward. Suddenly the Normans turned their horses, cut off the forces that were chasing them and massacred them so that no one was left alive.

'Twice this trick was used successfully, then the Normans attacked those who were left. The English army was still very strong but at last it weakened and the English suffered many deaths. Even the lightly wounded could not escape because the army was so tightly packed.

'As the daylight began to fade the English realised they could not hold out much longer. They had lost most of their army, the king and two of his brothers were dead. The English turned and ran.'

(adapted from William of Poitiers)

Harold's death.

38

Why did the Normans win the battle?

None of the records tells us exactly why the Normans won the battle. None of them tells us if Harold or William were good generals. We have to work out these things from what happened. Historians often have to do this. They find answers that are not given directly in the records.

What are *your* answers? Was William a better general than Harold? These points may help you to decide.

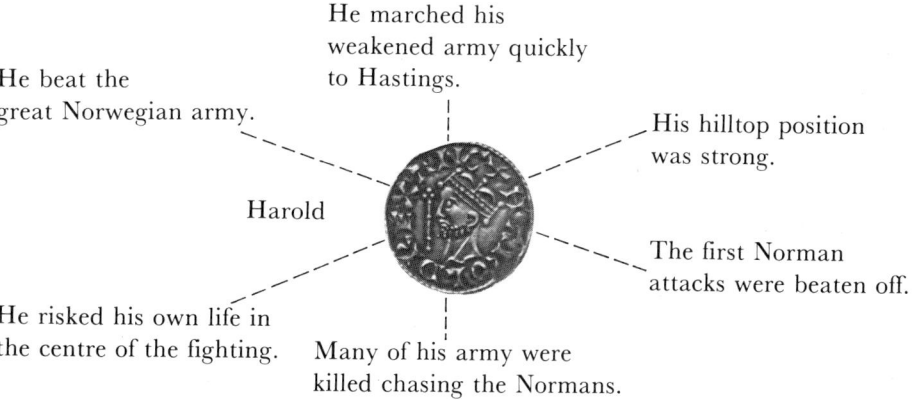

He marched his weakened army quickly to Hastings.

He beat the great Norwegian army.

His hilltop position was strong.

Harold

The first Norman attacks were beaten off.

He risked his own life in the centre of the fighting.

Many of his army were killed chasing the Normans.

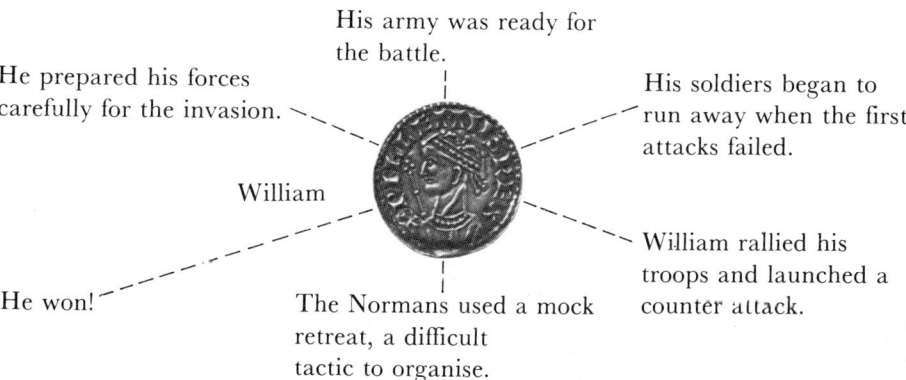

His army was ready for the battle.

He prepared his forces carefully for the invasion.

His soldiers began to run away when the first attacks failed.

William

William rallied his troops and launched a counter attack.

He won!

The Normans used a mock retreat, a difficult tactic to organise.

Are there any other points you would include?

So why did the Normans win? Was it William's leadership or English tiredness? Perhaps luck played a part. What other reasons could have helped to decide the battle?

Was one reason more important than the others?

Why did the Normans invade England?

We have left one of the most important questions until last. We have looked in detail at the battle of Hastings but why did it take place? Why did William want to be the Conqueror of England?

This is a difficult question to answer because the records do not tell the same story. So far some records have more detail than others, some are a little vague, but they have not disagreed with each other. But they *do* tell different stories about the background to the conquest. Why do they disagree? By looking at the English and Norman records you should be able to work out

a why the Normans invaded England,

b why the records tell different stories about the reasons for the invasion.

Edward the Confessor

Edward became King of England in 1042. Before that he had spent his early years in exile in Normandy. His mother's father was Duke of Normandy. He returned to England to be king only after his rivals to the throne died young. Edward knew and liked Normandy and the Normans. As he had no sons of his own it would have been natural for him to appoint his distant relation, Duke William of Normandy, as his successor. But would a foreigner be accepted as King of England? Much of the country was controlled by Earl Harold Godwinson and his brother. Harold was the most powerful Englishman. Why shouldn't he be king after Edward?

Edward the Confessor.

Family trees of the Kings of England and the Dukes of Normandy to show common ancestors.

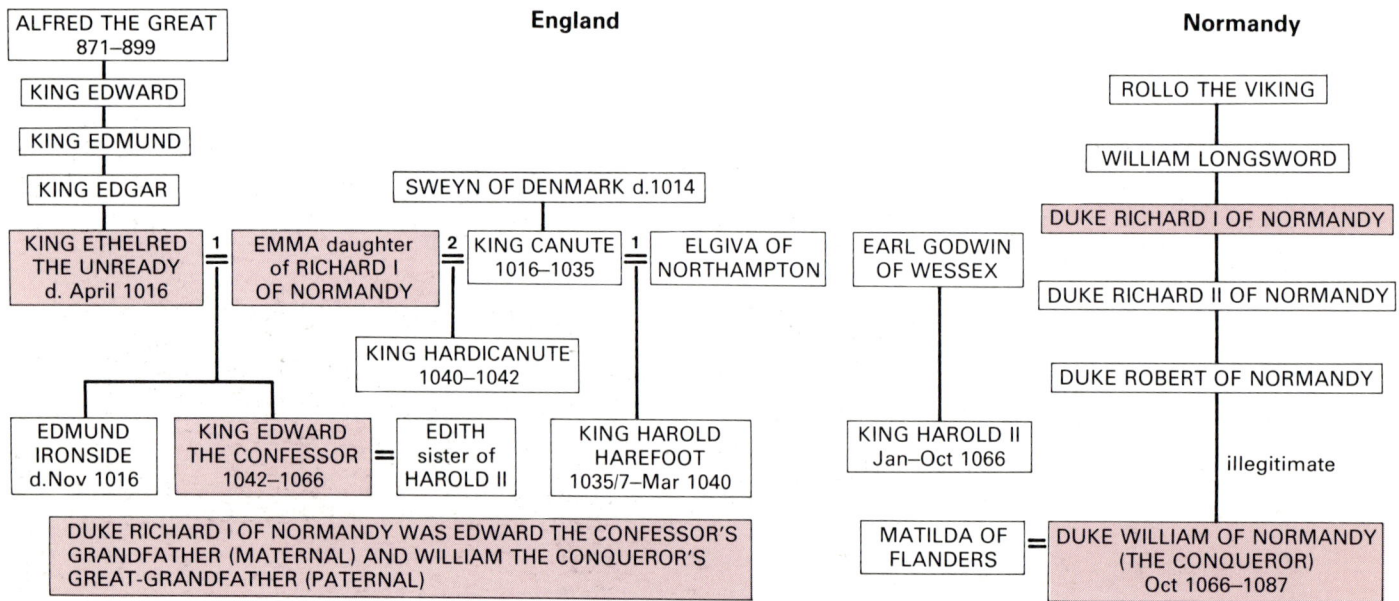

Area of England held by Harold and his brothers in 1066.

The Oath

It seems probable that Edward promised the English crown to William. As he grew older Edward was worried about the succession and so he tried to make certain that the powerful English lords supported William. He sent Earl Harold to confirm the promise of the English Crown. This is how the records tell the story:

The Bayeux Tapestry — After landing in France, Harold was held prisoner briefly by Guy of Ponthieu. Guy handed over Harold to William and Harold fought alongside William and the two are shown as allies. (William gave Harold a suit of armour.)

a 'King Edward sent Harold to William so that Harold could guarantee that Duke William would inherit the English throne. Harold stayed with the Duke and swore loyalty to him with many oaths.' (adapted from William of Jumieges)

b 'Edward loved William as if he was his brother or his son. He made William his heir and therefore sent Harold to William so that he could confirm this promise with an oath.'

c 'Many truthful and honourable people who were there say that Harold swore on oath — of his own free will. He promised that he would do everything in his power to make sure that, after the death of Edward, William would become King of England.'
(adapted from William of Poitiers)

Left: *Here William gave arms to Harold.*
Right: *The oath-taking.*

Why did the Norman writers include the story of Harold's oath? The English records do not mention this incident? Why not?

King Harold

Early in January 1066 Edward the Confessor died. Harold became king and was crowned. On these pages you can see the Norman and English accounts of how Harold became king. How do they differ? Why do they differ?

a 'In due course Edward died. Then Harold immediately seized the kingdom, breaking the oath he had sworn to Duke William.'
(adapted from William of Jumieges)

b 'Later there came the bad news that England had lost its king, and Harold had been crowned. This headstrong Englishman didn't wait for the English to acclaim him as King. No — he broke his oath by gathering together a gang of his evil supporters, and seized the throne on the very day of Edward's funeral, when everyone was sad at their loss. He was crowned king by Stigand in a ceremony that was not acceptable to God. The Pope had just ordered that Stigand should no longer be a priest.'   (adapted from William of Poitiers)

c 'After Edward's burial, the under-king Harold, whom the king had named as his successor, was chosen king by the chief nobles of all England. He was crowned on the same day with great ceremony by Aldred, archbishop of York.'
(adapted from Florence of Worcester)

d 'Earl Harold succeeded to the kingdom of England, just as the king had granted it to him and as he had been chosen as king. And he was crowned king.'   (adapted from the *Anglo-Saxon Chronicle*)

e: *King Harold on his throne crowned by Archbishop Stigand.*

As well as recording these events, some writers mention the appearance of a strange sight in the sky. Why do you think the 'long-haired star' was included in these sources?

f 'On 24 April a comet was seen, not only in England but it is said all over the world, and it shone for seven days with great brightness.'
(adapted from Florence of Worcester)

g 'In these days a star with three long rays appeared. It lit up the greater part of the southern sky for a fortnight and many thought that it forecast a great change in some kingdom.'
(adapted from William of Jumieges)

h 'Then all over England there was seen a sign in the skies such as had never been seen before. Some said it was the star "comet" which some call "the star with hair".'
(adapted from the *Anglo-Saxon Chronicle*)

i: *They wondered about the strange star in the sky.*

Why did the Normans invade England?

The Norman records give a very different story from the English records. The Normans said Harold had stolen the throne and had broken his promise to William. Did William invade England because he had been cheated and betrayed by Harold? Or was Harold the lawful king as the English records suggest? William might have wanted to be King of England because he had a lot of enemies in other parts of France. What do *you* think? What evidence can you find among the records?

43

5: Conclusions

Checking for bias

In the last few pages you have faced a new problem. The Norman records tell a different story about the reasons for the Conquest from the English records. Part of the reason for this difference is that the writers were biased — they each wanted to show *their* country in the best light. The picture on the right shows William of Jumieges presenting his story of the Conquest to King William. Why do you think William of Jumieges might have been biased?

Historians need to check the reliability of the people who produced records. Three questions they need to ask are:

a Who wrote it?
b Where did the information come from?
c Why was it written?

What other questions would you ask to find out if a writer was biased?

William of Jumieges presents his chronicle to William the Conqueror.

Unreliable records

Bias is only one reason why records may be unreliable. Look at these cartoons. Why would you doubt the reliability of these record-keepers?

Using records

Throughout this book you have been learning how to use historical records. Records have told us far more about the Battle of Hastings than relics could. But records bring problems as well as information. The cartoons below show three of the main problems you can face when using records.

Norman England

We have learned a lot about the Battle of Hastings from records. Records also tell us much about how the Normans governed England and so do relics from the time. On these pages you can see what kinds of effects the Normans had on England.

The impact of the Normans on Anglo-Saxon life.

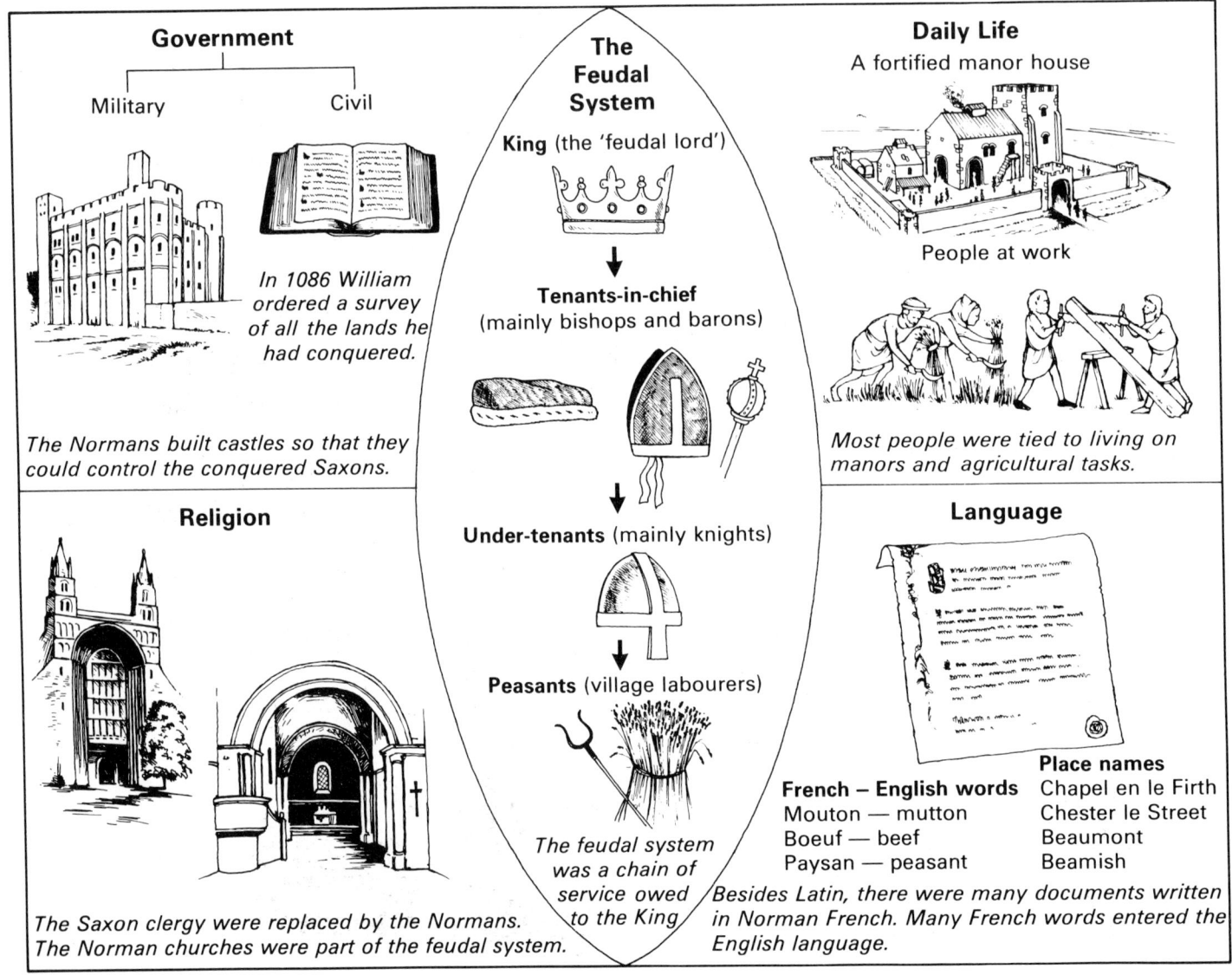

Government

Military   Civil

In 1086 William ordered a survey of all the lands he had conquered.

The Normans built castles so that they could control the conquered Saxons.

The Feudal System

King (the 'feudal lord')

↓

Tenants-in-chief (mainly bishops and barons)

↓

Under-tenants (mainly knights)

↓

Peasants (village labourers)

The feudal system was a chain of service owed to the King

Daily Life

A fortified manor house

People at work

Most people were tied to living on manors and agricultural tasks.

Religion

The Saxon clergy were replaced by the Normans. The Norman churches were part of the feudal system.

Language

Place names
Chapel en le Firth
Chester le Street
Beaumont
Beamish

French – English words
Mouton — mutton
Boeuf — beef
Paysan — peasant

Besides Latin, there were many documents written in Norman French. Many French words entered the English language.

Later records

Domesday Book is the best-known Norman record, but it was only the beginning. The Norman kings developed very efficient ways of government and these depended on good records. Record-keeping increased rapidly.

In later centuries the invention of printing increased the amount of records even more. Historians can find books, pamphlets and newspapers from the sixteenth century onwards, as well as greater quantities of private handwritten records such as letters and diaries.

Historians who are interested in more recent times have even more records to study. Their problem is to decide what to look at among so many sources — photographs, film, tape-recordings and computerised records all help historians to work out what happened in the past. But whatever the records are, historians must use them carefully before accepting them as evidence.

Left: *Anglo-Norman records*.
Right: *Twentieth century records*.

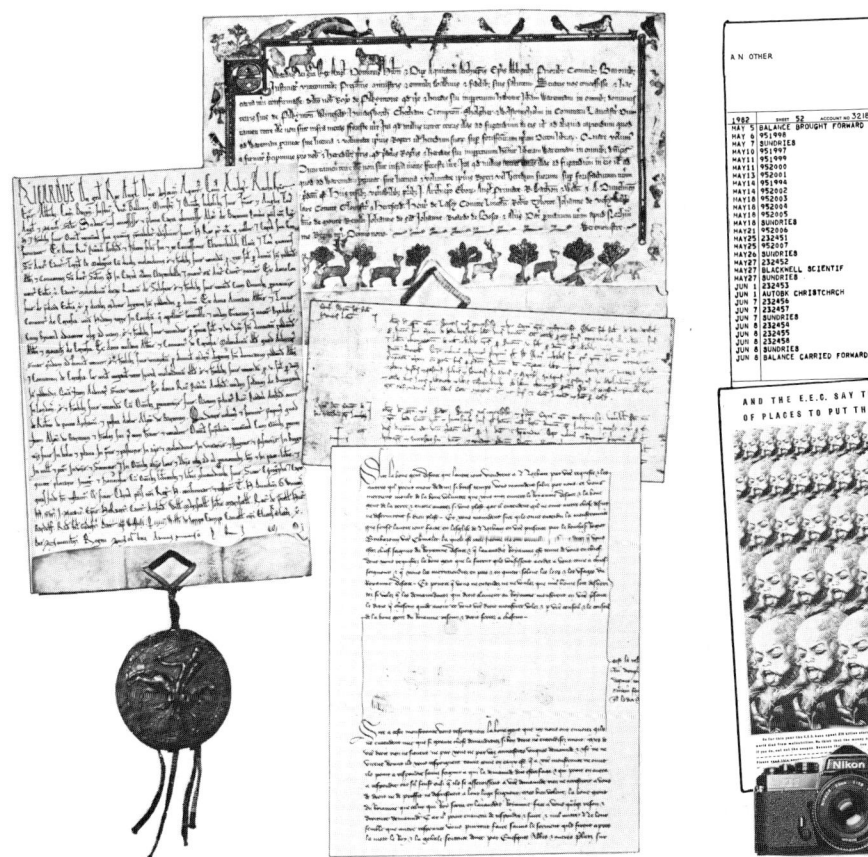

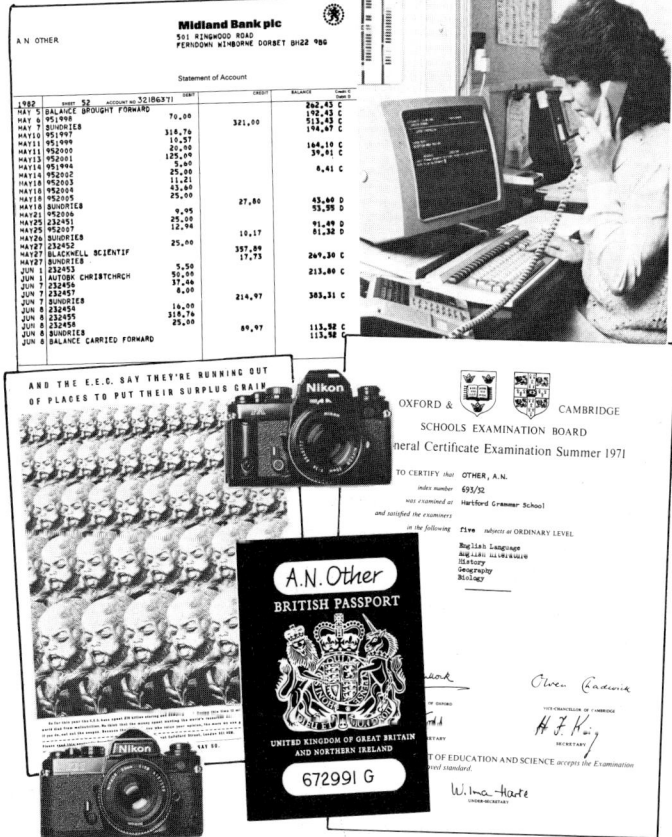

Making the most of records

Although records are sometimes difficult to understand, historians must use them. Historians cannot afford to ignore records that have a few gaps or are not very clear. They must use them very carefully. Records are compared and checked against each other. This is called 'cross-referencing'. Historians also try to check the reliability of sources. If historians are careful they can make the best use of records from the past.